The Black
Butterfly
My Unfinished Story

RENEE MURPHY-CLARK

WESTBOW
PRESS®
A DIVISION OF THOMAS NELSON
& ZONDERVAN

WestBow Press books may be ordered through
booksellers or by contacting:

WestBow Press
A Division of Thomas Nelson & Zondervan
1663 Liberty Drive
Bloomington, IN 47403
www.westbowpress.com
844-714-3454

ISBN: 978-1-6642-5735-1 (sc)
ISBN: 978-1-6642-5734-4 (e)

Library of Congress Control Number: 2022902380

Print information available on the last page.

WestBow Press rev. date: 02/22/2022

Contents

Introduction

My name is Renee, everyone who knows me, and if you know me, Nay-Nay is my nickname given at birth, born March 27th, 1969. A Washington D.C. native in George Washington University Hospital, I'm proud of my city, but today I will go only to visit. I am an only child to both my parents. Mom & Dad have both been in my life since I was born. I write this book not because I'm shy but because I want to just let it out, letting go of things I have carried around for years, things I have never shared openly with others, with allowing my children to live a life of freedom. It's okay to be yourself because you're the only one who's going to have to answer for it. Life has not been easy, but my life has been worth living. When I think about all the happy times, it outweighs the bad times. But I am profoundly grateful for the bad times because that's when I thought critically and grew as a person into a woman of substance and purpose. Today I am a mother of 5 children and a one-time grandmother, wife, and pet owner. I love these roles I have but realized one day I needed just more self-fulfillment. I raised my children, and I went back to school, got my associate degree, and now working on my bachelor's degree. It's my time now to find myself and see what I can and could be if I had made different choices in life previously. I pray that if you are reading this book; it makes a fundamental difference in your life.

> *Proverbs2:6- For the Lord gives wisdom; from His mouth comes knowledge and understanding.*

Dedication

First giving honor to God to whom all things are possible, Romans 11:36. I dedicate this book to my granddaughter Ava, my children; Bryant, Brandon, Shadae, Thurman Jr, & Teona, and my mother with loving memories of my father rest in peace dad.

To my children, it's okay to be vulnerable, but make sure it counts toward the next person and then yourself.

Love, MOM

> *Proverbs 3:27- Do not withhold good from those to whom it is done.*

Chapter 1

Fried Chicken

I'M MAD, ANGRY, AND FRUSTRATED AT MYSELF and my husband. Upset, mad because every time I suggest an eye-opening reason, something is occurring. Hubby thinks it's time to defend, speak up, and assume I'm reaching for a reason to blame. Angry because he, along with his defiant mood has caused me to be very nasty in my mood. I feel he wants to play the victim, and there's no need. Frustrated because I'm so in love with him it's hard not to give this problem some long consideration. I can't breathe, my chest feels tight, can't sleep, and it's 10:36 pm on a Saturday. Spoke with hubby over the phone, and while chatting I hear him say, "Give me my phone". Why does she have your phone" I asked? And he says she hides it from me, why I asked? But as I questioned this behavior, I can't think but wonder whose number is she needed or looking for, okay! My stepdaughter is 16 and has done the inevitable already. Stuff that would have gotten me killed by my parents and grandparents, aunts, and uncles. So even though what sounded innocent probably had a motive. My response was, whose number is she trying to get out of your phone? Or honey, she's trying to get a number. You better be careful or watch that. Many emotions break loose, and now what I'm saying to him and what he's saying to me is meant for nobody but us a private conversation between husband and wife. But why are you yelling and cursing me when I only gave you an eyeopener to maybe or what could be another attempt to add to her behavior roster of what she's capable of? I love my husband so much, my chest wheezes when we're apart, he's, my air. Yes, I'm asthmatic and incarcerated in one of VA's largest Maximum-Security Prisons for Women, Troy, Va. Cell #104. Lord, who knew this is where I would be at 49 for embezzlement with 54 felony indictments, 51 null processed, 25 years was the penalty. I'm doing 18 months with one1-year probation in front of me after my release. Missing everyone and everything I did when I was free. Every day all I think about is what I want to do when I get out, not to mention all the foods I want to eat and try again. With fried chicken being the first thing on the list. Oh, yeah, and kissing my hubby also, and seeing my mother's face and kissing her too. I'm a grandmother, and mother of 5, three biological children, and two God handed me. Yes, I am legally married, the love of my life. I know I love him because I pray for him daily about everything. Even though he runs my blood warm sometimes, I thank God for my husband because I know he loves me. Yes, he does. I am a handful too. Keep reading this book, you'll see.

> *Job 38:25- Who has divided a channel for the overflowing water, or a path for the thunderbolt.*

Chapter 2

Sentenced

1 0:38 PM IT'S A TUESDAY NIGHT, JUST FINISHED
watching "Haves & Have Nots" by Tyler Perry
on Own Network while sitting on the couch with
hubby snuggled up. A knock comes on the backside
door entrance of our home. King is running around
like a chicken with his head chopped off. King is our
Pomeranian and family pet. He lives up to his name.
This is an unusual hour for someone to be knocking on
the door, and yes, King is out of control at this point.
I answer the door. The officer says good-evening
madam, I'm looking for Renee Murphy Clark. I speak
up and say yes, that's. me, how can I help you? Hubby
says, who is it? The police I said. What? What do they
want? Me! The officer says, "We have a warrant for
your arrest". I beg your pardon, was my response.
Madam, kindly get dressed and go with me. I must

escort you to the county line to be picked up by the Nottoway County Sheriff's Office. He read me my charges, and I got dressed and was transported, too.

At the county line, there was another police car waiting for me and my husband in pursuit of our car behind me. All I could do was think what was going on felt like a nightmare. However, I'm nervous it's cold outside and raining. Once at the Sheriff's department, I'm told to sit down and wait for the magistrate. The handcuffs were placed on me, and fingerprints are being done. Thinking this is a joke, I'm being pranked, but this prank has gone too far. My charges are being read to me again. This time loud in front of a magistrate, and he immediately tells me no bound tonight. Take her to jail. This just got real. My response was, what do you mean jail? and I was being pulled out into a car heading to the jail in Farmville, VA? While my husband was trying to get questions answered and find out how we were going to communicate. I'm in disbelief, and so is hubby, thinking about how life can change so suddenly. It irritated my whole body on the inside, my head hurts, my nerves are out of control, and this magistrate just said what to me, who does he think I am? Is all that was running through my head? I know I did not just hear him say "no bound, goodnight, take her to jail tonight". In the back of another police vehicle, I went up another long country road in the rain, and it was freezing. Tears in my eyes, tears in my husband's eyes while telling me to hold on babe, I will figure out something. He's hollering you need an attorney and a bond. While the officer is walking around to get in the car, I'm thinking yes, I'm 8 days in jail now and we have an attorney, and I just made a bond. I'm back home for a year, and 7 appearances in court all returned another time. I just knew they were going to throw this case out of court, but oh no. The 7th time was the charm. The last day to appear was announced, and it's a Friday at 9:00 am. I am the only one in the courtroom except for my hubby, my mother, the judge, my attorney, and the Commonwealth of Va. Oh Lord, help me now, I begged, and I turn to see my accusers walk into the courtroom and take a seat. Judge says this crime carries 25 years max. How do you plead? 1yr of probation and a restitution fine of 32,000.00 dollars. I will give you 10 days to report to jail and get all your affairs in order.

Job 39:5 Who set the wild donkey free?
Who loosed the bonds of the onager?

Chapter 3

I Love You Dad

(RIP 2008)

LORD KNOWS I HAD THE BEST AND THE WORST parents a child could have, at least through my eyes. I am an only child and maybe a little spoiled, but understand they talked little when it came to discipline. A spanking did the talking, and my chores were done. I appreciated everything that was given to me. They taught consequences to me, and my mom and dad made sure of everything. They remarkably well kept and treasured me as an asset, meaning you don't spend the night everywhere, you don't eat everywhere people eat, and you don't sit in public toilets, you don't sit on anybody's toilet. Mom and dad were quite different but similar. Mom was a college girl, dad never finished school 8th-grade education only. I admired him after I got grown, and Lord knows I miss him now. My dad was a real man, a provider, a man who diligently worked, and a man who did not mind going to work. He would tell you to go to work or school. Yes, a man of means. My dad never cashed his paychecks until he knew he had another one coming in. There was a time he'd have 2 paychecks in his wallet, and we still ate plentifully. I never saw a late notice or an eviction unless they taped it to someone else's door. I had an outstanding childhood, and my dad provided that for me and my mom. Mom also worked. I'll talk about her later. Dad provided for us both very well. I lost my dad to out-of-control stomach cancer. The week we found out was the week he checked out and was ready to go see Jesus. Dad spent time in the Army and went to Vietnam to contract Asian Orange, a disease caught by men in Vietnam who were fighting. He tried extremely hard to get everyone ready before he left us. My father would leave an impression on everyone he met or knew him. His structure was enormous, and tall, which is where he shopped for most of his clothes. A straight-up guy with no chasing, and if the truth hurt you, he was effective. He would extend you his handkerchief and pray for you and himself. Stay connected to God Nay is what he would say to me. Lord knows I miss my dad more today than ever before. I haven't always gotten along with my dad because of rebellion. I didn't always comprehend a lot of what he was saying or what it all meant, because I was open-minded and opinionated, too, and maybe even judgmental. I am comfortable saying that today. Being exactly like a person you love to despise can be extremely confusing. Today I can almost recall some of our conversations. We never talked about the things I wanted to talk about boys, sex, tight clothes, and spending the night with my cousins. Dad was the head of the household, protector, and provider. He paid the cost to be the boss. I received the best and latest designer clothes, shoes, and toys always. It all came at a price. Chores that had to be done on Fridays and maybe during the week. My grandmother, my father's mother, cleaned rich folk's houses so well that when she retired, they still paid her until the day she died. Which was the guideline of my chores being done superbly. So, dad knew what a clean house should look and smell like, and he made sure our home stayed cleaned. Mom had asthma, and cleanliness is next to holiness, he would say. Today I keep a clean house, everything has a place, kitchen, and bathroom. I say a lot about a woman or person he would say to me, but it can't say much if you don't let people use them. That is what I thought but would never say aloud. By keeping your hands clean, stop biting your fingernails, or your face will break out. By the way, dad was a drill sergeant in the army and had a knee injury when he returned a stray bullet fragment.

Kissed the ground when he returned to US soil. How dirty was that I thought every time I heard the story?

God Bless those guys who served in Vietnam. It was hard for everyone involved and family members who supported our military during that time. Thank you!

I could never walk up on my dad as kids do. When playing in the house, if he naps during the day, it almost costs me my life one day. Mom was cooking Sunday dinner, dad fell asleep watching a football game, and I was playing on the floor. I got onto my dad's lap to play. If laid on his chest and went to sleep, he snatched me up and yelled enemy. Suddenly he recognized me and told me sternly to never do that again while he dozed because he would have to hurt me. I saw something different about my dad that day. He left Vietnam, but Vietnam had not left him. I thought what could have happened over there would allow me to see that look on his face I will always remember. He never mentioned it, and I never asked, but I knew to stand off him when he slept and never enter the door of my parent's bedroom. My mom is/at least she tries to be God's peacemaker, and on the other side of my story, dad gave me to mom when I was 13 years old, meaning I stopped hanging with him and became my mom's road partner because my womanhood showed up, I'm a late bloomer. If he hadn't taught me everything, he wanted me to know about life. Well, it's too late because it's her turn now. Dad gave me my rough edges, taught me how to fish, fight, stand for what's right and what's in my heart according to belief, how to work hard. Mom didn't always agree with his methods, but she never stopped him, either. I would climb trees, race the average boy in the neighborhood, with my dad making side bets on me winning. I was an ordinary daredevil. Watched Evel Knievel as a kid, and for every stunt he performed, if I could attempt it, I used my bicycle. Dad brought me 3 bikes in one week. I damaged them doing stunts and hit a parked car riding down a hill. Emergency room, here I come. But I had to show no fear, get up and do it again. He never encouraged the stunts, but he didn't want me to lose heart riding a bike properly.

> *Proverbs14:15- The simple believes every word, but the prudent man considers well his steps*

Chapter 4

Mom

BEAUTIFUL, SLIM, NICE BOOTY, HAIRY LEGS, long hair, and gentle spirit. She always smelled good, even at 75. Mom still dresses elegantly. She owns a million pairs of shoes of hundreds of shoes; my foot has outgrown hers now. Peacemaker, laid-back, easy-going kind of lady. Loves her family and yours. If she knew you. Mom is a gift-giver Christmas, her favorite holiday, even though it's her mother's birthday. I never wanted to share my mom with others as a child. I was very overprotective of her as my dad, but we had to because mom is part Cherokee Indian, and this was my fighting spirit. I tried my mom one day and pushed her to the limit, and when I tell you, I won't do it again even at my age today, tears come into my eyes now as I come into my honesty of a time when I took my mom for granted. That was a time in my little-minded world when I knew who I was and who not to mess with. I thought my mom was too tender to get mad, or I felt like she wasn't tough as me. But today I see who the tough girl was or is. She was the toughest of us all, and you don't realize this until you become a mom or parent yourself. We don't know our parents until we are adults and have children all our own. We try to put ourselves in their shoes and wonder why they don't fit. You know their names; you know what they expect from you as their child, but there are always closed-door moments. We don't know who our parents are until we are late teenagers or grown. Our parents grow up during their times in life and raise us according to how they saw/ see things or what's happening around them. When you're a parent, you must raise your children according to the time you're living in now. We try to put ourselves in their place and think maybe we would have done differently, but guess what? The times they lived in influenced the choices they make. So, either we clash, or we have family chaos, because when I raised my kids, my parents interfered, and that's cool. Being myself was how I raised them, from my perception of growing up with my parents' rearing differences from mine and how things are now. My parents whipped my butt. I screamed at my kids and gave whipping if the consequences called for a spanking. My mom had seen so much pain in my growing up and in her life, from being plagued by medical issues that she endured. She gave me the eye during mischief when I got caught, and if the eye did not fix your behavior, you are now in serious trouble. She learned to appreciate every day, and she showed it to me and others. Mom takes her time in everything she does, and you're not rushing her. Mom cooked, cleaned, served others. She never was eager for anything. One day, taking my uncle to see a lady friend, the brother I never had, and my bunk bed partner, we encountered a drunk driver who hit us on the passenger side of my dad's car. We're laughing, talking, and joking in the back seat like we always do because he lived with us for a while. There's no one in the world like my mom's brother, my favorite uncle. Late-night talks, laughing and him giving advice. We got yelled at by my dad, but we never stopped. My uncle was a ladies' man, and he was a true fan of Smokey Robinson, uncle was Motown ready, he used to live across the street with his wife in Detroit from Motown, where singers go to make music and get discovered it was called HITS USA back then. I used to spend my summers there. I loved the plane rides. We, we're hit so hard in this vehicular accident it threw my mom into the windshield, laying there with her legs in the car but her torso on the hood, everyone's jarred but what happens next? No one is ready for my dad. Does roll call? He says Nay, you, okay? Jimmy, you're okay, and my uncle says look at Ruthann Man. To see my mom hanging halfway out of the car is traumatic to me, and my uncle jumps out of the car, and my uncle is pulling the drunk driver out of the other car and beating this guy like he wanted him dead at that moment. When I could get past what was a crowd forming and the commotion that was going on, I went to my mom and talked with her while my dad was screaming & praying in a manner I had never seen before. With tears in my eyes, I was at that moment grateful my mom was alive, but when the ambulance and police got there, they had to call another ambulance to the scene because the driver of the other vehicle was beaten badly. To the point, they thought he was dead. My mom was a complete miracle, came home in 3-months with just a broken leg, bruises, and scratches. We went to court, and we won the case, and the drunk driver survived. I was 9 years old. My mom is and continues to be loved by everyone she meets, still sowing seeds of love. She's very straight forward especially. To people she knows closely. Believe me when I tell you heaven heard our praise. She still critiques me, and I'm 49 writing this book. If I had an opinion about what she does, I would stand off from her about 25 feet as to not get slapped. Mom is from the backslapping era of time. When she has slapped you, she's prepared to slap you again if your response to the first slap wasn't successful. An East Orange, New Jersey native, part Cherokee Indian and black born October 9, 1946, will hurt you.

When I hit DOC, she got her hair cut off, so I

Chapter 5

The Bank

ONE NIGHT, IT WAS EXTREMELY LATE. I WAS about 12 years old, and it was past my bedtime. Even though I was already in bed, I could feel my bed shake in a terrifying way to me. I knew I was asleep, but awake enough to know what I was experiencing was very real. I saw it and felt it too. A dark black shadow came from under my bed and hovered over my bed from the foot up to my head, never seeing its face, but only the image of its shape. I was already on my back. It snatched my arms up over my head and shackled me at the wrist and ankles, well it felt like shackles. I saw nothing, and it held my lips together because what would have come out of me would have been a yell for my mom and dad.

So terrified, all I could do was think somebody could help me please repeatedly, and immediately a light came from the left side of my room. I thought it was car lights because a window was in the place where the light kept getting brighter. Already terrified here's a spirit of what looked like an image of President Lincoln with a top hat that appeared standing at the window, as soon as this image appeared through the window the dark black spirit went quickly back under my bed, leaving and releasing me with shaking my bed as I focused on the clear white spirit image not sure what it wanted I could feel it came in peace and a calm came into the room, still afraid I looked down on the floor before putting my feet down on the floor I looked at the Abraham Lincoln image and it was sitting down in the corner like it had a chair, there was no chair in the corner, I asked am I safe it responded with a nod and said, for now, I hollered to the top of my lungs mama, daddy while running out my room and my mom met me in the hallway, she looked at me and could tell something strange happened, she flipped the light switch and there were no images. She believed me. I know because she was eager to call both my grandmothers. My nerves were a wreck and the way I astonished my mother, the look on my face she revealed months later. My grandmothers both after hearing me tell my mom what happened over the phone that night told her to teach me the Lord's prayer and make sure I knew it before going back to bed that night. A long night it was the 23rd psalm I recited back first, and now the lord's prayer, in less than an hour fear will make you do anything fast. I learned it and still know it today. The devil is trying to collect her soul was told to my mom by one of my grandmothers. But I had to make a choice one night soon because for about three days as the lights went off and my bedtime steadily approached, going into my room was scary. The Abraham Lincoln image never left my room, and only I could see him at night after being tucked into bed. I can say I looked forward to seeing the image, because it kept the dark image under the bed, but still extremely nervous as a child. I awakened another night to find that the image of Abraham Lincoln was gone, and the bed rocked; I had to pee, but I was not moving a muscle instantly. That black dark image came from under my bed, threw me back down on my bed, silenced me, and held me down on my back, unable to move or speak, only able to think of the name Jesus, Jesus, Jesus! Think it Renee, say it Renee, is all I could tell myself inside myself was recite the lord's prayer in my head were all these thoughts, with looking that thing dead on. It finally went out the window and never returned to my bed. I would lie if I told you I wasn't scared, never slept on my back again, not even now.

Ecclesiastes 11:7-Truly the light is sweet, and it is pleasant for the eyes to behold the sun.

Chapter 6

Telling A lie

MY DAD, HEY NAY, WHILE AT THE FISHING HOLE one day, he wished I was a boy, everything before me and everything after died. He wished I was a boy. To the point he says, what's this? I hear about these nightmares, nope dad, not nightmares, real deal stuff. Nay, girl, stop joking. Your mama said you were scared? said she has never seen such a thing. Your face was pale. Dad stopped playing. It was real. I learned the lord's prayer and the 23rd Psalms all in one night, both grandmas on the phone. I went to bed waiting to fight, and it never came back until 3 days later. Girl, that's a nightmare Nay, dad, it was real. It scared you, Nay? No dad, I lied. That's right don't forget those scriptures he said. You will always need them for the rest of your life, why dad? You have a purpose, sweetheart; you have a purpose that I might not be alive to see. But I know why you're here, so you're scared? I looked him in the eye and lied again, knowing he hated liars, no dad. All my life, I have hung on to my dad's words or the conversations we've had, whether we agreed. But I always knew he better not catch me lying. The dark spirit left something behind. I became the best at telling lies, stories. Whatever you want to call an untruth, I could tell it.

> *Proverbs 13:5- A righteous man hates lying, but a wicked man is loathsome and comes to shame.*

Chapter 7

Summertime /
Latch Key Kid

AT 13, I STARTED SMOKING WEED AND cigarettes in the neighborhood, looking at boys. I talked about everything with my parents, for this I earned their trust but never talked about what I was feeling or what I was doing around the corner. Even though they knew who I was outside with, they never would have suspected me or my friends because they thought I was too young. Mom worked in the government, dad a truck driver local and minor long distance all in a day's work. He was extremely late coming home or right on time if he had to pick up mom from a bus stop downtown. Metro was in the future of making trains and building transit for commuting but had not started the rail system yet. Government employees got off around 3 or 3:30 pm about the time I got out of school. I could be home by myself for about a good hour and a half. This is a lot of time for me, the latchkey kid. My grandmothers would call to make sure I was in the house and safe, and to start my chores, cooking, something easy, cleaning up so mom could start dinner and do my homework, maybe watch some TV. I had a brand-new Atari game system. First, gaming system to ever hit the streets, I would sneak company in the house to show off. Mom would eventually call before leaving work to let me know she was on the way. She would catch the bus sometimes all the way home, and it was quick. Smells in the house would always give me away. What have you been cooking? She would say when she entered the house, I smelled fried eggs and bologna sandwiches. Did you do your homework? Quick lie, yelp. Did you do your chores? Yes. You had this TV on? No, why is it hot then? I'm caught. I cut it off. I wanted something to watch while I ate. My sandwich was my response. She never told dad. One weekend, my dad was moving fast and had a lot to do one Saturday morning. I guess no one went out the back door behind him until I went out to play, and there was one of those 5-dollar pouches laying on the ground outside our backdoor entrance, which we use a lot for going and coming. No one walking up the street could see it. Out of curiosity, I did. But I saw it as I stepped over it. I looked around to see if someone saw me pick it up, including my mother, who usually runs behind me to say don't be late coming in. I picked it up and went around the corner out of sight from my home and the windows of the home. When I got to a spot where I could open the pouch, a voice came behind me and said you got weed? How do you know what this is, I asked? Because my mom's boyfriend smokes, he buys from your dad. He replied, Renee, are you dumb or what? I told him to shut up and then asked how they smoke it? he said come with me; I don't know this kid's name anymore, but we were outside friends and grew past his years, and he was younger than me. But he went in the house and got some rolling papers from off the table in a living room of his home, and we rolled what was called a joint and tried smoking.

That grocery store I mentioned earlier had cherries on sale loved some Bing cherries. Everybody knows these are the best. I got a big bag full and sat outside and ate the entire bag until I threw up more than twice. I wasn't buzzing anymore but had what people call the munchies. I kept my money because I had an allowance every weekend if I did chores. KFC was in my neighborhood, and I brought a 5-piece dinner box so that I could share. When I finally went into the house, I was sleepy and had to take a bath. Trust me when I tell you my favorite thing became weed, KFC, and cherries or grapes. The dark spirit left something behind.

> *Proverbs 27; Do not boast about tomorrow, for you do not know what a day may bring forth.*

Chapter 8

Incarceration

JULY 20TH, I HAD TO SURRENDER TO THE JAIL IN the county where I received my sentence, which was approximately 10 days from my trial date, it's a Friday morning, and I'm still preparing my mind, soul, and physical self, meaning I smoked a blunt before reporting at 8:30 pm to wrap my mind around all this, and I was praying Lord to walk with me in this place. This was how I prepared. I bathed to the point I did, not having to bathe for a few days with scrubbing and moisturizing, deodorizing, and wearing all white clothing, socks, t-shirts, long Johns, and underwear, all this in 3 layers. Hair washed and done up, placing my wedding band in a drawer for safekeeping, calling my loved ones at the last minute, and using the drive to the jail as an extremely tender moment spent with my husband and our two daughters. Upon reaching the jail, we laughed, cried, and played, knowing that this is going to be a long 2 years in prison for me, but all of us. During my first week of incarceration at the jail, I found out I could buy hot fried chicken every week. I thought, "Oh boy, I can do this time easily". 2 weeks incarcerated, I found out I'm almost dead, feeling weak, staying to myself, and not realizing I'm breathing mold.

When do we go outside? I asked, what days do we go to the clinic? Because I'm not feeling well, every time I see a guard, they see me as a troublemaker for asking questions.

Noticing my mood is changing, and I'm sure it's not because I'm stuck in a closet with 32 other women, in a 50 x 30 space with 3 tier bunk beds. Something is happening to me. I'm calling home every day, but life's great because I got fried chicken at least once a week. But I'm using my asthma spray more and more, the rescue inhaler mainly. I never ate the food from the kitchen. I had a commissary account. I would not feed my dog from what comes from that kitchen. Nausea set in about week 3 now, and I have no appetite. I'm weak and can barely move, but I am being asked to move to another cell where there are more women, but privacy cells as well. I'm being noticed, having not moved all day by guards and cellmates alike. What's wrong with you? Someone asked, but when I turned around to answer, I was being rushed to the clinic of the jail, where I was told I was mold-infested, and almost died. So here I am waiting for the state to pick me up, and the county jail is killing me behind mold infestation. It cut me a break. I hollered at my Lord. Seventy women to one toilet. Are you kidding? Me, and 4 phones on the wall for us to make phone calls. This must be what depression feels like. I'm thinking, this can't be happening to me. The reality of jail was setting in and going to prison was almost a treat when considering I can go outside and eat better food and maybe make a decent phone call. I prayed, Lord, please don't let this be my demise, and instantly it seemed like my body reacted to the antibiotics they were giving me when they felt like it. In 3 days, I started feeling like myself and praying not only for myself but for others. Thanks to the girls in H-Pod, I will never forget they found me places to sleep, moving me further and further from the biggest parts of the repainted mold-covered up. Mold was still present, but I breathed a little fresher air, as opposed to sleeping next to mold every day and night. As for medical, they pacified me with Benadryl and eye drops.

> *Proverbs 25:28- Whoever has no rule over his spirit is like a city broken down, without walls.*

Chapter 9

Prison Time

To God be the glory! Because one night in the awful jail, the guard came to me and said get some rest; I said for what? Being a night owl, I like to read at night. I was told it was time to go in the morning incredibly early at 5 am heading out to the state penitentiary. I thought, thank you, Jesus! When I got to prison or prison intake, I knew that the hand of God was upon me. The first week in prison, I saw every kind of doctor being well kept and fed, not to mention I was on 3 antibiotics to stay alive. I never would have prayed to go to prison, but it thrilled me to go. I felt like I was alive for real. Today I am grateful for that test. It reminded me of what lurks in the dark. Jail time almost killed me, but prison reminded me that my time has begun and I'm closer to going home, even though I had another year and 8 months to go. I could wear real clothes in prison. I had a clean bed, a desk, a light, a better commissary, and a place to think, along with the opportunity to start this book. Being incarcerated has reminded me that the so-called comfortable life I made for me and my children is a blessing, and you realize that when you're forced to live against your normalcy. I'm blessed, and I know it. I'm grateful for what God has done in my life, and today I know this one thing is true because today I act as I know it. I have received God's mercy, and now I show it. Thanking God for prison and Jesus, who's the reason for all my second chances? If you have committed a crime. Yes, jail/prison is the place for you. I might have made it sound better than jail, but that's all it's better than. I want my gravy, the lifestyle in which God allowed me to have, and when these doors open for me, I'm running out the gate. But as for now, I am where I am supposed to be for the edification of righteousness. Everything has a season, and this is my season to reap understanding of knowing sometimes, you must walk alone to be worthy of a task. No, not everyone goes to jail/prison, but not everyone is as hardheaded as I was. God gives the needed discipline to those he loves.

> *Ecclesiastes3:1- To everything, there is a season, a time for every purpose under the heaven*

Chapter 10

Hubby and I

HUBBY AND I HAVE BEEN MARRIED TO OTHER people before, but nothing beats being married a second time to the right person. If this were my 1st marriage, I believe I would not have done it again. I would not have considered being married twice. The first marriage was a total flop for me. It warned me in a dream to not marry this guy, and to be honest, out of spite and desperation, being convinced about the ticking clock thing, a woman getting too old and your clock ticking, stupid.

Okay, so doing a lonely period in life and somewhat enjoying the single life, I started dating a guy who's not serious, but it was fun, and it had convenience, no attachments. I met my hubby, and out of respect for a close relative, he kept his distance. I consider the other guy a bridge to my happiness. However, we were around each other, often laughing, sharing, and bonding with others, while double dating. My husband became incarcerated during our time as friends for about 5 months, and that's when I broke it off with the other guy. A collect call came in, and it was my husband at this point. We reminisced about the times we dated and kept in touch while incarcerated, making sure I wrote him often. I would always answer his calls when he called, and one day I informed him of my goals and plans for life. To my surprise, he was on board. After getting out of jail, we talked and hooked up as a couple. After a few weeks, we were engaged, to be married 2-years later. No one knew because we had to work out some details, like getting to know each other on a different level, to make sure this is what we both wanted. I knew my husband's children, but what I did not know was they were his children. I used to engage in the Angel Tree Christmas program that had names attached at the mall. I chose his kids, not knowing they were his kids, and giving them at Christmas. But after we got together as a couple, the introductions started, and to our surprise. I knew them because I brought them school supplies. After knowing them previously after Christmas, there was another organization for school supplies. It was a drive started by the county. 3 years later, the wedding of our dreams took place with our flaws, laughter, and tears. We both would not have had it any other way.

After 3 years of marriage, we brought a Pomeranian to commemorate our anniversary from a breeder, and his name is King. We normally go to Las Vegas or some other resort place and laugh until it hurts, and the rest is adult stuff, lol.

> *Song of Solomon 1:2- Let him kiss me with the kisses of his mouth, for your love is better than wine.*

Chapter 11

Life's funny / Renee

IT'S A GIRL ON MARCH 27TH, 1969. I SAID EARLIER I got my rough edges from my dad, but when I think about it, they both should teach me how to be me. Brains and wit, along with common sense, on a whole different level of thinking and acting. By showing me what was around corners and dark alleys, maybe they thought that would deter me, but they were right for a while. It never stopped me, because they showed me how to fight and protect myself when not in their eyesight. My parents made me a visual learner, maybe not intentionally, but if I saw it, I either wanted to go closer. If I didn't, I stayed away from whatever I saw. Life's funny, because I gave birth to three children, and I did the same when raising them on my own, showing them how life can or could be with choosing visual aids in our environment. Consequences we learn early in life, whether we understand why we develop a certain type of comfort zone parents should provide for their children. As we get older, we decide if this is what we want to maintain a standard for our parents. What I mean is if they taught you to wash your hands before and after you eat normally, this is what you pass down to your children. If you do this still, to see someone not do this makes you uncomfortable because it has become your norm. Currently, after being incarcerated was not my problem, it's the folks in prison that are. This journey has caused me to question myself, my purpose, and what am I to get out of it? Lord, what am I to see? Why me? A booger-picker, people who walk out of the bathroom and never wash their hands, folks who are just trifling like my roommate, I thought I would explode, but I quickly remember the consequences of being placed in confinement and not being able to see my hubby on visitation or hearing my mother's voice. So, I kept my hands to myself for fear of losing privileges, so I slowly talked my opinions about fear of my belief in what I believe. I also have allergies and asthma, and the stupidity of others trying my patience causes me to blister or rash up. I might have a mood swing that changes my attitude because I don't have a tolerance for ignorance at all. I want to be doing something, even if it's just sitting quietly for the moment. I enjoy the silence. Many people don't understand that, but I'm cool with it. I don't like it

Chapter 12

The Logging Truck

O CTOBER 21ST, 2005, I'M GOING TO MAKE A BANK deposit for BP gas and truck stop rest area at around 9 am. As I approach a curve on a one-way road, meaning one lane up and one down, I see a tractor-trailer heading towards me. I'm going northbound, he's going southbound. There are two guys in the road fixing a car with the hood up on their vehicle, and the speed limit is 55. I must swerve around them to keep from killing them, and back into my lane was the tractor-trailer. Immediately, all I can do, hear, and remember is the bang of the truck when it hit me. I remember seeing a black dog lick motor oil off my feet, but no one else seems to have seen a dog, nor was there any information about the dog in the police report. I was losing consciousness and traumatized to the point I was in shock, according to the report, after realizing my femur is broken. Watching the black dog was my concern. I was losing consciousness fast. I remember thanking God I was alive 10 days later after the third surgery. Yes, I won my case, but nine surgeries later and five therapy sessions after the surgeries and lying on my back 8 months in hospitals/ rehabilitation centers, I remember saying thank you to Jesus daily. It appeared time slow down for me to think of God in a way I never thought of before, other than when my daughter was born in 1991. Not realizing the miracles that took place while I was morphine-induced for days out of my mind, I have no recollection. My parents had to decide not to amputate my leg, or who would watch my children while I could not? My hip busted, my femur was obvious to see, my knee crushed, and my tibia broke. I awakened to realize 10 days later that I had had 3 surgeries, and I coded twice. A heart murmur was detected, and now I have become anemic. Today I have my leg, and some days with the help I need to take my time due to pain. Some days like nothing ever happened, no pain meds rarely, some days I can feel bad weather coming. I never wore a cast, only five fixators at different times to stabilize my left leg until they performed other surgeries. I had two of the most successful doctors anyone could ask for. I thank God for them both. I knew they were God-sent when appointments came around in their office. Credentials posted, and the testimony they give about me being a patient is clear. People traveled from around the world to be seen, and I'm glad they chose me on the day of my accident to fix my left leg. Praise God! I wrote a testimonial, and they featured it in a medical magazine titled "God Favored Me," considering the work they performed during my surgeries. The worst thing about my car accident was losing a friend during this horrific process of healing, who was also my son's godmother. Breast cancer was winning a battle with my good friend, who was military and flew from Korea to be by my side with praying and anointing my leg daily for at least 20 days. I miss you so much, J.H. Rip in peace, my friend.

I had spent many days asking God why would such a thing happen to me at this magnitude. The moment I got the nurse from the school of hard knocks, I stopped asking, and then she returned. Again and again, she was an excellent nurse, but mean to me, I thought. To this day, I pray for her because a part of me loves her, and let me tell you why our first encounter, she says to me, how are you feeling today? I said, how do I look? she says not my question with the look of ponderousness on her face. I feel awful was my response. She said looking and feeling are two different things, so which is it? In a snarly voice, as she untied my straps, which held lines and tubes out the way, and she was also preparing to bathe me, speak, she said, and the tears poured out of my face like waterworks, oh now she said what's eating you? And suddenly I felt like we were playing a game, and like a child, I gave up because I knew I had no physical fight in me and was helpless and needed her to help to lie on my back. Over a month, I was being examined for broken glass that might have been in my hair and skin daily as she cleaned me up. I humbled myself and wondered if this was a dream, no it's not. Feeding line and IVs in my neck and arms, no use of my hands because I was combative. After the nurse was done, she cleaned like new money, being gracious for her and the help she provided. The why my question again comes to mind, and then the answer was, why not you? I suspect God was telling me I'll show you better than I can tell you because I cried a lot of days and nights, and I became broken not just physically, but spiritually, and that nurse was the sandpaper to start the process. She was a definite part of the healing process. She treated me better because she was very tough and caring, most of all patients and in thrall. Her ability to remain firm with me is what I needed because I was the problem, not her. When I humbled myself, she became the nicest person I had ever met. I looked forward to her visiting me, even if she wasn't my nurse for the day. The day came, I had to say goodbye, because she was called to work another wing in that hospital, realizing they use her for the difficult patients, an Angel used by God to bring people to their truth.

Ephesians 4:16-17- From whom the whole body joined and knit together by what every joint supplies according to the effective working by which every part does its share causes growth of the body for the edifying of itself in love. This I say, therefore, and testify in the Lord that you should no longer walk as the rest of the Gentiles walk in the futility of their mind.

Chapter 13

My Children

I LIKE TO THINK I'M A WONDERFUL MOM, OVER-protective, but I love being a mom. I feel I did my best for my children. I did not allow them to not be children. But made every attempt to give them a childhood I would have liked. We had open-door conversations. Nothing was off-limits if they had questions. My second-born child would probably beg the difference, but he's a Marine today, and that's cool. He has a little PTSD, but I'm proud of him like any mother would because he sacrifices every day his life for others. Stubborn and bull-headed, but what man isn't? He just thinks differently than I do, and that's cool to see he has his own mind for a reason. He's also a trendsetter who deals with that middle child syndrome, where enough is never enough. Things must be his way or no way at all, or it could be the Irish in his blood. Murphy is black Irish, which is what my dad was. I guess I'm the same way having things my way, so he keeps his distance from being a workaholic for our military. Or it could be I throw things today, it could be we might kill each other, but we usually find common ground and hold safety to have a conversation. I'm thankful for that, but he knows, and he assures me love is what we will always have for one another. We can be hot or cold. I pray for my son every time he deploys, and God has been faithful always with his return and the new attitude he displays lately. This is a blessing. So proud to be a Semper Fi Mom. My heart spreads wide to anyone who has lost a child to sacrifice in our US Military. The rest of this page is for you. I love you Cornbread, but you know this already!

My oldest child is an instructor who's my power of attorney because my life is an adventurist. My son keeps me on my toes, he's the brains of intelligence part of me folks don't know about. He has style and grace and is a definite trendsetter. I spoil him rotten but holds two degrees for that. I'm proud he believes in teaching strangers everything he knows and why they should know everything he knows about cooking and haircare. Very witty and exotic type of guy. He's my hairstylist and backup cook on holidays, as well as owning a salon with partners and cooking for events, yes remarkably busy. I try hard not to bother him, but some days I just can't help it. Answer your phone feeling frustrated with him. It's me calling your mother! Hahaha, I love you!

My daughter Shadae; is named after the singer, but spelled differently Sade, but sounds the same. My beauty, my innocence, my gift from God to the world. Waking up to her is a blessing. She loves me unconditionally, and she receives the same love back from everyone she meets, especially from family. When we all come together (Before Covid), everyone takes their turn doing stuff for her, distant relatives jump in to do whatever needs to be done.

My daughter is bound to a wheelchair, and as an infant 6-days old, she contracted the chickenpox, not having anything toward them of it off. Praise God, my genes were strong enough to help her fight what could have killed her. She is 27 years old today and going strong. However, she's on a muscle relaxer. Her only medication for spasticity was to catch that first seizure in time to prevent more. Her neurological damage was the delaying of her nervous system, which doesn't fire as it should. She has a high school diploma. She holds the Jacqueline Hyatt award for achieving hurdles in life that seemed impossible, like her 2yr degree. Yes, we sued the hospital, and she's well taken care of. I love you! Dae-Dae! I educated myself on her condition. I trained every nurse that ever worked with her in our home. My daughter smiles about something every day, all day while incarcerated. I hear her smile over the phone while envisioning it.

> *Ephesians 5:13- but all things that are*
> *exposed are made manifest by the light,*
> *for whatever makes manifest is light.*

Chapter 14

Still Blessed to Be a mom

AT, LEAST ONE OF MY STEPCHILDREN IS A LEGAL adult. He's moved out away from home, got his place shared with a cousin. I'm proud, we both are. My husband asked me to mother his 2 children before we were married and planning on getting married and I said I Do before the dos. He gets on my nerves, being so good to me. He is mister-right for me. My husband had two of the sweetest sour patch kids who fit right into my world came along with this relationship another boy and girl now I have 3 boys and 2 girls who are now the babies and my family made them so welcomed and brought them up to speed and date with showing them love like I had given birth to them. They had another set of everything in their lives, from grandparents to aunts, uncles, and cousins. So, like with any other ready-made merging family, we had to learn each other's ways likes and dislikes hurts, and fears, and work through them like any other family, but you can best believe God was the center of that circle. Today I'm a mother of 5 and I'm proud that my 2 angels had a mom. She was the portal that brought them to me. For that, I dedicate this chapter to you, RIP Monica. I never knew her. I mothered those 2 kids from ages 6 and 8 as though they were mine by buying them everything they wanted after their chores were done. Taking them to the Malls movies riding adventures to the point they were tired of traveling. I know they would say, mom; we tried. How long is the ride hiding nothing from them, having talks they can use with their children one day? Teaching them things only a mother would do and teach and yes, they got disciplined too by me because what we not going to do is tell me my place when you're out-of-place now; you had no problem spending my money your way if I said clean that room; I mean clean that room or there are consequences & please no back talk. They know me and just like my 3, those 2 don't always agree with me. But they know what and how to approach me and what they can get from me if they come correct, meaning no childish mind games, they get what's true coming from me with that mind game, and if they need it; they got it if they need and want it. Oh, I got leaves that need raking every year. During football season, regardless of any disagreements going

Chapter 15

Teaching

I LIKE BUTTERFLIES, ESPECIALLY THE BLACK ONES. They are the teachers of the cocoon, one black butterfly per cocoon. The life expectancy is short for a butterfly. They serve their purpose and die like humans, so to speak the black butterfly is the teacher of the entire cocoon its purpose and when it's done, it dies while the others live. My dad always hinted around that I would or should be a teacher before being incarcerated. The first lady at my church told me she has a class. She wants me to teach. She'll start it up when I get out. But long before that, I felt like I have always had those abilities and techniques to teach with being a mom, a wife, and an In-service worker on the job medical field, to me these are confirmation that maybe my dad saw something in me. If I learned something, I had no problem teaching it to someone else. Teaching to me is giving another person insight. I get a thrill watching a person light up after a revelation is no longer a mystery of the unknown. What I don't like it when folks want you to think for them, especially when the opportunity presents itself for self-improvement. I always wanted to be the first to teach my kids, people including my mom would tell me why you are having conversations with your kids about that. My response was, why not? I want them to know the truth, so when they heard it again or got into a discussion with others outside my presence, they could make their conclusion with what I said and what they heard. The more a person knows, the further a person goes in life, or the possibilities to become greater are endless. The mind expands to create ideas; I believe. So, I was 1st to open a world of possibilities or discovery up to my kids and if the family was lacking; I shared one did not have to ask. I was called Ms. Know-it-all my parents made me read a book. My dad was this person for me growing up I admired my dad he was a self-taught kind of guy who only had an 8th-grade education but could negotiate to buy a car, buy a home, and teach me how to balance a checkbook, pay bills, and read a book, importantly a bible. He also owned his boat. A tractor-trailer driver and charter bus owner local and long-distance. He won several driving awards along with doing on-the-job training for new employees within the paper company in which he drove a tractor-trailer.

Romans 12:6- Having then gifted differing according to the grace that is given to us, let us use them if prophecy let us prophesy in proportion to our faith.

Chapter 16

Teenage Life

I WAS 14 YEARS OLD, AND I WAS PREGNANT he pulled my pants down and laid me on the bed boy I went to school with when it entered me, and as he touched my body, I went through something I knew was or should not be happening when I got up and pulled my clothes up and left to go home I walked into the house and I no longer felt like the little girl I was, that morning when I woke up I felt like I needed a shower. I screamed and yelled for my mom to come into the bathroom. She saw the blood and said, honey, it's okay, that's. normal she assumed my menstrual started and I could not tell her different. I got into the shower scrubbing his scent off me and 5 months later my parents found out I was pregnant and became frantic my dad wanted to kill him, my mom, at a loss for words but before they knew I was pregnant, I ran away from home for a day. I was back home that night because of a good friend whose mother went to go talk to my parents first. Life changed drastically. After that, our lives changed. Daily, my mom and dad played the blame game, and I'm not taking off from work to take her to the doctor. The arguments continued for a while; they did not believe in abortions but sometime later in life I had 2, they never knew. Four months later it's a boy the son they never had I got a lot of stuff from the emergency room and labor and delivery staff of that hospital because I was the youngest mother on the ward, like a major baby shower in the 3-days of being hospitalized. At home, the arguments between my parents were thick and I could not help but think it was all my fault for having this baby. A baby whom I loved so much who now shares my loneliness, I thought during these times; I held this baby, and it held me too. When my parents aren't arguing they would come to hold my baby at different times and they would move to another room of the house to spend personal time with my baby either outside, or in the living room, babies change people I thought because their moods changed after some days and weeks went by. I can tell they love him because the arguing is over and it's more directed at me now. The county we live in has provided me with a school tutor, so I graduated on time and went back to school on that yellow bus. After graduation, I went straight to full-time work and paid for a babysitter.

Chapter 17

Bored While Incarcerated

BEING INCARCERATED, I HAVE MET WOMEN from every background. I can and cannot imagine the stories I have heard. Where these women have been and what they have endured has gotten me to a point. I'm so grateful I had my parents, and I lived the life I did growing up. The obstacles that some of them still must endure are scary still to this day. I believe the worst is the stories from women who have small children that must be are raised by someone else. Because moms are in jail/prison, but life happens. Not to mention the drug stories and being co-dependent, they bring the same habits to prison or in jail. Family members or friends send money to the commissary and that money is used to buy drugs, which is the coping element that helps them get through all the time they must serve. For me, it became this book and calling home as much as my money would allow along with reading my bible daily and watching my surroundings because you trust no one in a penitentiary; I have transferred to 2 of them, and nothing changes, but the scenery of this one I'm in now is a maximum-security prison. The age group varies in all of them, and the food is ridiculous. I'm bored, but I brought a TV but mostly, I need to move around, and I'm not allowed until the walls closed in, and after a while, you don't care if you're breaking the rules, you just move. I held the job of mopping the floor while in prison; they shipped me to all of them too. I dedicate the rest of this page to Toni Nanette Hartlove, who is a transgender and the first to be in a women's maximum facility in the state of VA. I learned a lot from Toni and when she would notice my behavior or my ability to not follow the rules, Toni would pull me to her cell and converse with me on life. She made sure I got it right while being incarcerated; we shared a bag of commissary cashews when she revealed her story to me after I read it in a Richmond times news article, and I disclosed it to her I wanted to write a book and she encouraged me to tell my story it's yours she said. Live it, tell it, and don't do stuff you regret. Like getting yourself in trouble being in here.

This place is not for you, she said. Thanks for being a listening ear, Toni,

Your Friend,
Renee.

> *Matthew 7:1 Judge not that you be not judged.*

Chapter 18

Secrets

SECRETS CAN CONTROL US. THEY CAN MANIPULATE the way you think, live, and react to others. Being unconscious of this can make you wake up one day and change your perception of life. Secrets can influence your character, personality, and humane persona of how or why you do or don't do for others or yourself. Secrets can result from how you raise your kids, or they can determine why you like red Kool-aide as opposed to purple why you choose a particular spouse or mate. We can either grow stronger or better, or we can allow a secret to overtake us and sometimes kill us slowly. Some secrets can destroy families forever and friendships. For this reason, we form secrets because of what others will think or do and the way they react. So, we carry secrets, or should I say baggage, for years. Some families sweep it under the rug because this becomes a norm until someone trips up. This becomes a part of our lives, unwanted heavy baggage that we can choose not to carry. Let it out because it filters those unwanted negative things that cause you to not be free.

> *Romans 14:11- For it is written; as I live,*
> *says the Lord, every knee shall bow to me*
> *on every tongue shall confess to God.*

To my kids, my husband, and my parents for making my story worth telling, for giving me a story to tell, I have grown into a better person based on learning from each of you in your walk. My husband, I plan to ride this out till the wheels fall off whom I love until eternity. To my girls, Shadae & Teona keep dreaming and never stop pushing and searching for what's real. My sons, Bryant, Brandon, & Thurman Jr. continue until you create a legacy that you can be proud of.

The End.

Printed in the United States
by Baker & Taylor Publisher Services